Field

Harriet Tarlo

Field

Shearsman Books

First published in the United Kingdom in 2016 by
Shearsman Books
50 Westons Hill Drive
Emersons Green
BRISTOL
BS16 7DF

Shearsman Books Ltd Registered Office
30–31 St. James Place, Mangotsfield, Bristol BS16 9JB
(this address not for correspondence)

www.shearsman.com

ISBN 978-1-84861-511-3

Acknowledgements
Parts of *Field* have appeared in *Fire* magazine, 2011, in the colophon
series, 'Asterisk', from Fewer and Further Press, U.S.A., 2011 and in
'Open Field: Reading Field as Place and Poetics', *Placing Poetry*,
eds. Skoulding and Davidson, Rodopi 2013.

Field

Penistone 2008-2011

At Pangeston (at Domesday, 1086), then Pengeston, Peniston, Penistone, the highest market town in England: a field seen by any train traveller heading in and out of town on the 29 arch viaduct over the Don. (*Pen*, Celtic for hill, here the great ridge between the Don and the Little Don).

10 Oct 08

it's the Huddersfield side
of Penistone which is
the spectacular one

31 Oct 08

    that field
— patch of scrub
      tree clump
in the middle —

           murmuring in train, shift after
               Penistone folk   get on

28 Nov 08

railway mornings,
three stations in, the
moment of passing
the field, heart raises
head to sight it, winter
sun crossing
   it, wanting to ₁
      walk it diagonal
     desire (drag-mire, myne, FP)
to be   daylight

7 Dec 08

match box standing in
    sideways, small power
sheep slowly walking
    the lee of the wall
winter dawn exactitude
    waiting for the field
come — and — gone

10 Dec 10

train slows down
      coming into Penistone

waterlogged strips under sun
      trees cast shadows
back the way we've come

               pheasants in corner
                  running to woods

               flicks of green through
               trees – sun full on
               face

30 Jan 09

The Plan — to stop at Penistone /
get off / cross over / head back toward
Denby Dale / facing tracks /walk
to your right / new houses edging
the Don / on the other side: the field
find the farmer? change perspective?

13 Feb 09

shape changes as it grows
    down to water
    up to road

        take path's route down
            open and obvious
      but allowed?

15 Feb 11

early mist	head throbs
on cold glass	strains
eye to see	field
consumed	catch
tree shadow	is it?

16 Feb 11

growth under glitter
sun   tyre tracks
glisten   green   putting
on inches it almost
seems   spring   light
crops   rising   field

dull again at 4.00
reflecting grey sky
back through green
curves still tint light
little tilt back from
behind cloud edge

24 Feb 09

looking for the field
starting at Pen. Station
beep beep beep
reversing insistence
scratty out of town
house-building, not
stone, pale bricks
orange bricks

walking along
the line, the way
the train comes in
(electric plant, old light
industry, blue tits
        threading
winter branches
little sign of green)
and back, taken
a wrong way

early spring song
against machine

11 March 10

tired, waiting
for the field

tall tufts of grass edging wall
stones across field-width

then   a heron
still, on marshy scrub

We just call it the swamp field – you know that lump of swamp in the middle you have to plough round. I don't know if it's got another name. (AH)

12 March 10

warmer and wetter spring

falls, field still barely

green

how it drops away

down　— almost a kite

the stone wall, a central spar —

muckheap midway

ends silver-wet track

under earth to field banks at river edge

not sharp, but rounded, rolling over and soft

down to the Don below

24 March 10

misted lightly over

pale new build
up to bank-
edge over
Don

orange-stained
balconies
hang
over

shiny silver squares
stapled in to stop
riverbank slump
when people live
up there

holding land
up

27 March 09

"my field"   that is not mine...
that is mine, it is so near to the heart, RD

    stand up to see

    the field – working out

    a line

                it's planted

    up – couldn't cross it

      anyway

    maybe

27 March 10

at the last viewing field hazy

    through filthy windows

feverish to find out by foot, car, train

permission is not found in

place

28 March 11

growing goldening muckheap

grey pigeons tree-side

fine day — pattern flow —

train shadow rolls through

field

3 April 09

the crop has grown
around that scrubby
patch   seems now
space contained, boarded
by river, roads and houses

was that the feeling
of the end of grass?

4 April 2011

waiting for
          appointed place time nexus
   between The Dark Peak and The Yorkshire Coalfield (AR)

      train a ladder across
   one window on hidden field systems,
      one on faded steel works, foundries

  a moment when

          people stand high, in the lee of
          the wall, on Penistone Station
             train displacing wind
          about their hair

   it's a huge view isn't it, from here,
   up there?

1 May 09

rape sprouts at the top
green (wheat?) below
rising uniform down
to boggy valley bottom

     turning to look from the other
     side of the train, estate houses

                    Penistone Reinforcements
                    Wire Manufacturers Since 1959
     light industry   what fields
     were there

          pylons sent the scale
      right out

11 May 11

swelling blossoming rape
            rolling the angles
sweeps   marsh patches
                    empty angry
           scrub between
a change of colour
              first yellow
                    the end of green

13 May 10

purple earth between
   green gradations
buttercup ridge, different
   yellow
      scale and
white (stitchwort?) stretches
   away on far bank

it's all go in
      illumined grassland, LS

13 May 10 (driving)

take South View, Stayley Royd Lane
up past Hullock   deep frost on Nab side
              but bright and clear
Scar Hole Lane, Windmill Lane, cross
Hey Slack   sheep grazing
              in the morning
                        uneven capstones stark against
                    sun

into cut and speed of morning route
through High Flatts, Ingbirchworth
right turn to Penistone
....

from Barnsley Road
it's boundaries, not
field that's seen

we are the top line, cars
glinting in sun, tiny from train
seeing right over unseen Don
to Spring Vale cement works,
houses, school
              church above

turn down, skirting it,
park up field-side, lorries
jolt-juddering down-bank

wheat a good 12 inches now
rape, patchy, a few feet
over the wall, bees
hovering

nearside, stones subsiding,
patched with stake fencing
wire rolled behind

        conservative billboard
        fixed to fence

far side, post and wire
barbed over, trails
down to hedging

        hawthorn, elder

dipping below
to ditch or stream?

. . . .

bank rises as you descend
the hill, head under bridge, left on
Water Hall Lane, the house fenced off
from new build, its barns now
little cottages   [PRIVATE]
behind gates

walk into the park: white spirea
cow parsley patched with blue
pimpernel, forget-me-not; frost
beneath carved conifers
cherry blossom scent
and birdsong

in bramble, nettle, under
cuttings and embankments
the last dripping viaduct arch
behind wired, re-wired gate:
the field-bottom, running twisting
river dark-lined with oak-birch
remnant

once sediments *folded, eroded*
tilted, uplifted (AR) into long-time
hillside   till walled around
within   tree boundary planted
(from here, seems 4 not 3)
              stones buried, fallen
under season's cover
              wheat so close, wet with dew or
              melting frost, rape a small
              triangle up
              above

train over my head
screeches into Penistone

*The ditch down the side of the viaduct — BR are
meant to maintain it and keep it running clearly
— but they don't look after it and it spills into
the field.*

*My grandfather tried to sue them — the company
that put the main sewer in running right under
the land — for not putting the land back right —
but they'd gone bust.*

(AH)

Sometimes, if we go low in a field (physically, lying
down, or just being in the lower part of a steep hilly
Yorkshire field, such as the Penistone field, the horizon
is within the field or we are within the horizon, the
fold: **a field folded.**

        field's slide line down
                light depth of sky's
        blue white   it is something
        is it

shifting slightly every second
the field line crossing the
sky diagonal horizontals
across a dizzy moment
of slide
as we surf the rails

            swallow skim over crop cover
                    yellow sprinkle
        cushion crop billow lines

3 July 09

misty after days of heat

the scrubby patch marshy

orange-pink at the centre

(like a painting, JB)

what flowers leaves

that colour?

rickety row of new build up

on edge above

builders tinkering

10 July 09

the crop crossed/cut through
where vehicles went & go but
growing – undulating up & down
            around what's left unploughed:
rough path, marshy scrub, three trees
taller than all

            at intervals an animal
            has lain down — perhaps —
            a small patch of crushed
                  wheat, is it?

            or just the wind
            patterning?

20 Aug 10

what?   I never saw
is it a wild thing?
        what, so fast, JT

black dog joy
running top field

           man
    at the edge
      calling

calling his dog

she won't come
    back
not now she's in

13 Sept 10

heap spread all over
field, doing quiet work:
all ploughed out now

8 Oct 10

today the mist
is such, there is
no field as such

13 Oct 10

yellow sprayer, someone
sorting it out: first time
figure in the field

We only started ploughing it five years ago – up until then it was permanent grassland or had been since long ago – five years ago we had a yen to put a plough through it – we tried a new crop of grass first, thought if it can grow grass, we can crop it – my grandfather never remembered it being ploughed before. (AH)

The lines of the plough remain through the seasons, at times crossing
each other, circling around the central swampy island
curving at the edges of the field to form wide
loops, a calligraphic imprint
into earth

20 Oct 10

evening

> unreal light
>   angle onto
> field projects our train
> riding over the great
> stretched arches

> flickers kestrel wings
>   hold-fluttering

puts near-full moon
into pale shadow

25 Nov 09

wind-blown rain hits side-on – sun &
rain again – waterlogging field bottom

floods in Cumbria

rivers bust their bridges up

this part is terrifying at night cause of all the trees
and the river, you can't hear anything except the river

says Penistone girl crossing the tracks

leaves blow back past

as we go

18 Dec 09

morning

snow-falling, not quite settling
— fugged up windows —
        field: muck pile in the middle, growing
again, still living

evening

at three on a winter's day
shadows creep up field
from Don

5 Feb 10

on Penistone platform, just up

from cold white field, the faces —

their hats and bags and laptops

guitar, umbrella, bike —

wait to be sprung off

to Barnsley, to town, to Meadow'all,

to work

| GRIT SALT |

10 Feb 10

patterns of ice over

dark water in low

field dip

darkened trees, wet against

white furrow lines

seem to deepen

into earth

12 Feb 10

waterlogged:
    rain washes
snowmelt
down
    into soil:
air stops at water
    slides down
        ridged water
seeing it obscure
    in wet window
clinging drops on glass
    close condense
the warmth we inward
    produce

5 March 10

sun so light
it's hard to see
the field
                    frost- line
                    path   ice puddles
                                      melt in
                                      morning
          tree shadows cast
          towards us, over
white marsh

          ----

                    the way home
          expecting nothing — till
                    a heron and shadow
          pick over pool though
                    there seems to be no sun

10 March 10

red in the field
tiny bright tractor
pulls trailer slowly
down-track, dumps
load on midden pile
drives back

does this happen
every day and I
not see it?

The Muck heap is for the field – we'll spread it on there. This is a NVZ – Nitrate Vulnerable Zone – you're only allowed so much muck, only allowed to keep it in places not near watercourses, to spread it at certain time. There's a fair slope, but it would all go into the soil before it got to the river. (AH)

12 March 10

still silver lines traced
wet downfield in
emergent sun

> by evening it's a pool at
> bottom – duck mates
> ripple-swim tandem

16 March 10

few streaks of snow

across earth

    starlings fly on

over, a flock

    over the meltwater

grey low wet of

    field bottom

pale houses unreal, for

    sale, above

Now one, this field was six small parcels after
The Penistone Inclosure Act 1819
Awards thereunder dated 28th Jan., 1826
Allotments here awarded under the Penistone Inclosure Act
in lieu of tythes.

The enclosure and sale of commons in the liberties mentioned
under the various Inclosure acts passed since 1807, and the
awarding of allotments in lieu of common rights, greatly reduced
the number of keepers of Penistone sheep.
(JD, 1906)

*My grandfather created one big field from three. You have
to grow your fields in size – especially with the price of
diesel, you need a long length – turning round, that's what
loses you time and money.*
(AH)

23 April 10

it turns into planes of light and
shadow abstracted, that old enclosed
pattern of field parcels, land
handed out for
tithes
    walls on walls making
this "landscape" little
rectangles right over the
West Riding (240, 239, 246, 247)

We keep finding old wall bottoms

27 April 10

morning

        sun

    does field exist in
heart as a necessary
  high (point) to
journey   or the way mind
     shapes a structure
          from the allocated
            hour

beautiful morning, like summer
            beginning spatter yellow

27 April 10

night

        lurching over —
             beneath us, the thin
                viaduct
      can't see the edges of
        what we are on   without
   craning over suspended
     rush

at night   feel it under   see
       carriages flex twist   slowing, would fall
           to field

               once it did

30 April 10

misty in morning
rain — field almost
steaming   top corner full out in yellow now
        just four days growth (rape? brassica?)

below, what might have
    been grass is now a
    crop coming on

        sludgy mud about
        the pool where seedlings
        don't grow

....

evening, over-heated

    dull outside
  those three trees in a line
    (remnant? boundary?)
hidden traces   stand up against green
        through growth

21 June 2010

evening

    unploughed swamp patch
ring about it
    full of buttercups

23 June 2010

elderflowers float open, white
>
> between road and field

top corner glows last
>
> light, late afternoon

where the rape was, green now
a new crop

trees meet each other
>
> in full mesh mass

seems bumpy today

crops uneven, pathway

more of a zigzag

the rest so wet

and dark, it's almost

blue

7 Sept. 10

field ploughed right down
    to dark earth
    and shining lines

crop-shadow still where
the late crop was

trees (were they 3 or 4?) cut down
    to stumps, that patch
            left a scrub triangle

quick erosion of all that is
    distinguishing

2 years on, look up
    I've missed the field
        it's gone: there's Pen Station,
the blown-spattered people
          waiting

             bird arrow over
                  shifting sky-shape

15 Oct 10

now in wet dusk

clear green

colour

Penistone — bleak up here — I'm surprised it's still here,
surprised it hasn't been wiped off the face of the earth
says man on the train

there is a change, there is a change in all

      misty morning, that patch of scrub
      cut into by the plough, part-planted
      even

      flatter field
      without

      still growing

5 Nov 10

field much the same as the
other day, really
much the same

leaves blow in, scattering
blue-grey floor
of train

evening

everyday so shattering
people sleep going
home
        the field almost
in darkness, car-stream
at top of Barnsley Road
shift-lights it

10 Dec 10

       loving it again, the field
pink streak of sunrise above
         snow scaling down
irregular tracks of feet (whose?)
       trailing it

       the scrub patch rises
above snow crust ground, is
redefined   original land?

evening

       by night, the field top
green-dark at dusk shading along
        walls, down to low
riverside: thaw's come

16 Dec 10

snow again

coming home early

darkening short day

field light-laden

under darker sky

veering on to viaduct
lean over metal window
brink   its edge-stones
under us border
the far down
field

early morning pink horizon
lights up wet land
catches stump flats

Notes

AH: Adam Hinchcliffe, farmer, Penistone

AR: Arthus Raistrick, *West Riding of Yorkshire*. Hodder & Stoughton, 1970.

FP: British poet, Frances Presley

JB: British painter, Julia Ball

JD: John N. Dransfield, *A History of the Parish of Penistone*. Penistone: James H. Wood, The Don Press, 1906.

JT: British painter, Judith Tucker

LS: American poet, Leslie Scalapino

RD: American poet, Robert Duncan

All other italicised text is "found speech", unattributed, by railway passengers.

Printed in May 2022
by Rotomail Italia S.p.A., Vignate (MI) - Italy